D1539041

A Legend of Alexander

and

The Merchant and the Parrot

Books by Herbert Mason

The Death of Al-Hallaj: A Dramatic Narrative
Gilgamesh: A Verse Narrative
Summer Light, a novel
Moments in Passage, a memoir
The Passion of Al-Hallaj by Louis Massignon, four volumes
    (translator)
Two Statesmen of Mediaeval Islam, a study
Reflections on the Middle East Crisis (editor)

A Legend of Alexander

and

The Merchant and the Parrot

dramatic poems
Herbert Mason

UNIVERSITY OF NOTRE DAME PRESS
NOTRE DAME, INDIANA 46556

Library of Congress Cataloging-in-Publication Data

Mason, Herbert, 1932–
  A legend of Alexander ; and, The merchant and the
parrot.

  Adaptation of Iskandarnāmah and three poems from
Maṣnavī.
  1. Epic poetry, American.   2. Alexander, the Great,
356–323 B.C.—Poetry.   3. Sufi poetry, American.
I. Mason, Herbert, 1932–   Merchant and the parrot.
1986.   II. Nizāmī Ganjavī, 1140 or 41–1202 or 3.
Iskandarnāmah.   III. Jálāl al-Dīn Rūmī, Maulana,
1207–1273. Maṣnavī.   IV. Title.
PS3563.A7923L4   1986   811'.54   86-40338
ISBN 0-268-01281-4

Manufactured in the United States of America

FOR JEANINE

Contents

Two Views: An Introduction

The Mediterranean epic tradition, built upon Homer by Virgil, Dante, Milton, and Goethe, is a sequential architectural structure; it recalls and it projects; it builds a world view on world views; it assumes the authority of survival; the modern-day novel sustains its idea of wholeness but not its same interdependence.

The Mesopotamian journey epic is sequential in an older, more primitive, unVirgilian way. Its world view is implicit; its eventual deciphering is by those who see their own lack of assumed survival mirrored in its own; its idea is sustained by fragmentary consciousness; it is not a whole conception.

The Mediterranean views ruins as monuments, the Mesopotamian as inevitable consequences of erosion.

In one death is the incident that tests excellence; in the other it reveals impotence. They are not incompatible visions, but the Mediterranean is paradoxically both more modern and less sophisticated; it builds to an increasing ideology of the triumph and tragedy of will. The hero's willfulness is considered the substance on which survival depends and the basis of the epic's heroic affirmation.

In the Mesopotamian epic—which has appeared at even rarer times than the Mediterranean: in Gilgamesh, the legends attached to Alexander the Great, and those assimilated by the Semitic Bible and the Koran—the substance on which hope depends is grace. The hero's will is terminal; he drifts toward salvation by the winds, by Ultimate Reality, not by his own gifts. In the evolution of the epic, this Ultimate Reality

1

is not fate or chance or coincidence but conscious intent, grace, mysterious Personality. The hero's hope is not his will but the response to his desire from beyond himself by Another Presence.

The Mesopotamian is a religious epic, the Mediterranean an epic of civilization.

In the Mesopotamian, civilization collapses and the hero journeys from ruins to a realm without buildings; his efforts to construct his own salvation fall to further ruin. The source of ruin is in his own incompleteness: ultimately he is not the creator of the kingdom he seeks; the kingdom without death is beyond his invention.

In the Mediterranean, death is glorified in order to exalt the will. It is a tragic vision. The Mesopotamian is a tragic revelation of the end of the will from which humanity alone, not any of its creations, survives. This vision is much the oldest yet also the more sophisticated. There is something naive and obvious in the Mediterranean, wise and elusive in the Mesopotamian. Both recognize the profound consequence of loss, both are architectural acts of recollection and hope made in times of profoundly felt loss, yet the Mediterranean constructs a defiant work of denial, the Mesopotamian surrenders to revelation. Both reenter the worlds of their loss—the Mediterranean to relive tragedy in more concentrated dramatic forms, the Mesopotamian to live by accepting the ultimate failure to save. The one immortalizes the structures of this world, the other knows immortality exists only in the world to come. The epics are conditioned by the seas and rivers that surround and buttress or erode and undermine their monuments. But each is a survival in which many human minds and hearts see reflected to the edge of time the desire that is inextinguishable in themselves.

The Alexander and Khidr story, as I attempt to retell it, is written as a narrative of contrasts and interweaving testimonies of these two beliefs.

The narrative can be traced in terms of its personae and

their mythical encounter to the twelfth-century Persian poet Nizami, whose celebrated *Khamsa* includes among its "five epics" an *Iskandernameh*, a journey account of Alexander the Great and his companion-cook Andreas in their mutual quest for the spring of eternal life. The journey is fulfilled for Andreas, who becomes el-Khidr, the Green Man, one of the four immortals along with Elijah, Idris, and Jesus of the Koran; but Alexander seeks in vain.

Their encounter was conceived, then as now, for the historic force of Alexander's personality, his memory, and his heroic desire; and for the contrasting perspective of Khidr, whose values and calling are centered elsewhere than in worldly culture and self. We can identify the former without difficulty. We can understand the latter, not by "going Eastern" and even less by "studying myth," but by encountering a somewhat deeper yet quite sober orienting point within ourselves. They are contrasts in world views and world hopes, with Alexander being the doubting protagonist, and Khidr the relentless guide to eternal life.

It is a narrative for two voices. Khidr has encountered his celebrated companion in the Land of Darkness and is taking him to the Spring. The two men are dressed in robes, one green, the other gold.

A Legend
of Alexander

ALEXANDER.   Why do we go on this way?
    I know I'm going to die
    By my disease or by some treachery.

KHIDR.   We have a destination.
    Why do you think we're lost?

ALEXANDER.   We seem no further than we were.

KHIDR.   I know the way.
    What are you afraid of?

ALEXANDER.   Nothing, I've never been afraid.

KHIDR.   Some men are afraid of heights.
    Suddenly a ridge
    Along a roadside
    Makes their chest tighten,
    Their lips grow white,
    They sweat across the forehead.

ALEXANDER.   I will not sweat from heights.
    I used to stand on walls
    Too narrow for two men to pass
    And look down to the shouts of "King!"
    I never was afraid of falling down,
    And no one tried to pass.

KHIDR.   Are you remembering someone lost?
 A friend? Your wife?

ALEXANDER.   I lost my friend. My own Patroclus died.
 It isn't honest to grieve too long.
 My wife, Roxane; I was too old to love that one.

KHIDR.   You are still young in years.

ALEXANDER.   In time not counted by my years
 But incidents I am quite old.
 I've traveled far with Homer at my head.
 Old men have touched my hands and knees
 And pleaded for the bodies of their sons.

KHIDR.   Of enemies abroad . . . ?

ALEXANDER.   Home or abroad, it is the same.
 There's no escape from jealousy and vengeance
 Once you have crossed frontiers.
 But I am not afraid of minds
 That hate the inconveniences of travel
 Or dread to learn what others think.

KHIDR.   Of death, then?

ALEXANDER.   This *is* the last encounter, isn't it?

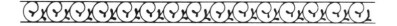

KHIDR.   Your quest is for eternal life,
Not for a cure for death.

ALEXANDER.   They are the same.

KHIDR.   One may become the other
But they're not the same.

ALEXANDER.   I've never been afraid of death.

KHIDR.   But of eternal life?

ALEXANDER.   I've seen too much of death
To think that life should be eternal.

KHIDR.   We're looking for its Spring.
It is a place where deathless water flows,
Where no one dies who drinks,
Where life is lived forever.

ALEXANDER.   An old man doesn't want to be
Eternalized as old
Or a coward as a coward.
One wants to die, the other to face death
Bravely.

KHIDR.   Each wants new life.

9

ALEXANDER.　　Another dream, another fantasy.

KHIDR.　　It is a well. We'll know it when we're near.
　　It is a place where pilgrims go
　　To touch its stones.
　　The stones retain their imprint.

ALEXANDER.　　I've heard of wells that cure.
　　Soothsayers speak of them.
　　But can it cure or dull
　　My pain?

KHIDR.　　You will gain new life.

ALEXANDER.　　Just cure or dull.
　　I'm asking very little.

KHIDR.　　You're delirious.

ALEXANDER.　　How else would I believe
　　We're on a journey to eternal life
　　When we have barely moved?

KHIDR.　　We have moved very far
　　From where we were.

ALEXANDER.　　I doubt your cures.
　　I hate your condescending simple talk,

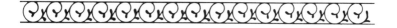

You're treating me like a child.
I'm Alexander, Conqueror of the World.
I *never* can forget that fact.

KHIDR.   You want to.

ALEXANDER.   I want to be regarded as a man
In your mystic twilight
As I have always dealt with men as men
In the full glare of my day:
With honesty, not lies
And spiritual deceptions.
You're cheapening the truth you seek
By hoping I will yield myself.
Take me as I am, don't hope I change.
These waters cure or give new life
To one whose heart is bold, not less himself,
Or they are just deceptions. I'm still on guard.

KHIDR.   You're still yourself.

ALEXANDER.   And will be nothing less.
But my mind is crumbling. I can see its walls
Collapsing on all sides. I know it's evening
Yet the light has not diminished.
It burns like noon. My throat is dry.
I can't remember if Granicus was first
Or Tyre. Why did I raze Persepolis?

11

What had the Persians done to me?
Or were they just the enemies at hand?
Is it my mind's or a city's walls I see collapsing?
I can't breathe; it's suffocating here.
The smoke from those fires is in my lungs.

KHIDR.   We must move.

ALEXANDER.   We can't move. You're lying to me again.
I know I've lost the power to move.
Do you know why I killed?
Because I liked it, you think?
Not at first. Because I wanted space to breathe,
Space to make my vision of the world take life,
Because that vision was the best, the one whose excellence
Gave greatest honor to mankind;
And men aspired in me, indeed conceived themselves in
    me,
As one who could achieve their aspirations.
That is it. Yes, that.
But, then, I tasted it—the terror in another's face:
The lips grow white, the forehead sweats—
You know the signs yourself—
As you replace his view of man with yours
In a single stroke. You terrify.
The name of Alexander terrifies! I am the terrifier,
The merciless, the never indecisive,

12

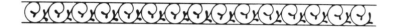

The one who gives the peace of death.
Old women, scholars at their desks, boys in the street
Recall the color of my hair, the way I had
With servants, horses, words . . .
The tautness of my legs as I rode Bucephalus,
My way with women,
My arms as I strung Odysseus' bow
And cut the Gordian knot—
All publicized my image to the world.
Everything but this. This is never told:
He was a wretched sufferer,
A bad friend to his guide
Who led him through Delirium,
The Underworld of the Diseased,
To further life.
And why? Why do you bother?

KHIDR.   I have no reason.

ALEXANDER.   Then you're the only one I've ever known
Who has no reason.
Perhaps you hope to publicize my weakness
When I'm dead?
To tell the coward's words I say
In my delirium?
To profit like a gossip on
Another's wretchedness?

KHIDR.   I don't have anything to tell.

ALEXANDER.   Then tell nothing.
    No, tell all.
    The world is best when no one has illusions
    He can be a god.
    Tell how I writhed and cursed and soiled myself:
    Say "You would not believe the foul smells he made!"
    I curse, I moan, I soil myself.
    I fill the night with cries,
    I who ruled the world,
    Or dream I did,
    Am like those bad travelers who dream
    They are all kings at home
    And only sufferers abroad.
    Hard talk, Khidr. We must have hard talk.
    What strategies must we plan for tomorrow?
    What will appearances achieve that actions can't?
    At last the great man is unmasked
    And all you see inside are little formulas—
    That worked.
    But you, Khidr, now you will think that I
    Who may not be the worst the world will know
    May serve as model in some foreign poet's mind
    Of what is still redeemable:
    That part that sees how badly I have soiled myself.

False hope, mankind. I should not be a mirror,
No one's mirror, not even mine. Why do you care?
You do care, don't you, if I soil myself?

KHIDR.   I am your guide to the sacred well.

ALEXANDER.   Why can't you find it?

KHIDR.   It is here. The way is known to me.

ALEXANDER.   You are being metaphorical. I want facts.
This mind needs facts.

KHIDR.   I know the way. That is a fact.

ALEXANDER.   You know why I have never trusted soothsayers
Or physicians or astrologers?
I couldn't trust a prophecy
Its prophet couldn't test upon himself.
More wise men died than heroes
In my company.
I never could be fooled — Beware! —
Except by innocent young soldiers
Who believed
That faith alone could win a war.
I hate wise men.
Their hearts are too impure
To serve beside these innocents.

15

KHIDR.   You served?

ALEXANDER.   I'm teasing you with words.
    Where is the sacred well?

KHIDR.   Ahead.

ALEXANDER.   Always ahead. How far? A parasang?
    The length of a hippodrome?
    Can't you hurry us along?

KHIDR.   We are approaching it.
    It takes some time to reach.

ALEXANDER.   Is there another way?
    Aren't you a curer, a physician?
    Have you no power to mix herbs
    To spare me this agony?
    I want to return to the light of day.

KHIDR.   I have no magic cure.
    The sacred well gives life.

ALEXANDER.   I wish we'd never met.

KHIDR.   We did.

16

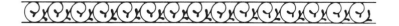

ALEXANDER.   A fact. Another fact:
   I don't want eternal life.
   The world I've known is here.
   I've been defined by it.
   I have no other place.

KHIDR.   Perhaps that place is nothing.
   Perhaps your exploits are forever lost.
   This is your journey, that is not.

ALEXANDER.   I can only seize on facts.

KHIDR.   This sacred well cannot be seized.

ALEXANDER.   My soul is just a memory of war.

KHIDR.   Desire for life.

ALEXANDER.   My soul is small not large.
   Shriveled, mean, closed, tight.

KHIDR.   Enlarging, too large for the world you've known.

ALEXANDER.   I have to know the evil I have done —
   My disease is glory for myself.
   I have to die or I will be *too* proud.
   There is nothing you can do to spare me death.

My mind is without walls or windows,
Nothing but loose rocks in a barren field.
Maybe two or three are still together,
One above the others, a rough shrine
Put there by an admirer.
I can't escape this paradox:
I want your gift of life;
But I want to face my death.
I'm out of all control.
My friend Patroclus died for me.
I can't betray my friend
For mediocre hopes of life.
Yet I want you, my physician, to tell me there's a cure.
Is my disease so rare it can't be cured?
What will it take for you to work to find it?
Give up this nonsense of the sacred well.
The time you waste on that is better spent
In finding cures. We're short on time.
The sacred is outside our competence to judge.
But cures are not. Consider my body not my soul.
The world I've known is what I ask for now.

KHIDR.　I'm not a physician or a soothsayer, but a guide
　　　Who was shown the sacred well. I am the one here now,
　　　Not someone else. You asked for honesty and truth.

18

I've told you who I am. There is a well.
It is a fact, not a metaphor to keep you journeying.
It must be reached. It has been found.

ALEXANDER.   I feel only the contractions now.
Where are we going? To what place?
How far through memories are the stones
That cover the well? You drank there?

KHIDR.   Bathed and drank.

ALEXANDER.   That made you green?

KHIDR.   My name is green. You call me green.

ALEXANDER.   The water is cool and fresh
To stop this burning in my flesh?

KHIDR.   To give you life.

ALEXANDER.   Not Lethe, not forgetfulness.
I want no artificial sleep.
I want to face my death
Like Homer's friends, Patroclus and Achilles.

KHIDR.   Not asleep.

ALEXANDER. Full consciousness. I must be conscious at my
    death.

KHIDR. It will be less than life.

ALEXANDER. It must be *more* for life to rise to it!
    Death must be *more* for men to be afraid!
    Men must be made afraid if they're to live.
    Death must be more. Life must be less. Life grows
    With death. That is the argument for death.

KHIDR. The argument for life is sacredness—the well;
    It will renew itself. It will *not* die.

ALEXANDER. I am contracting. I am dying. I am not
    Alive to fight.

KHIDR. We are near the stones.

ALEXANDER. Hurry. Can we hurry. Is there time?
    Why do I remember those I sent to death?
    They had no hope of a guide, no sacred well.
    What of them? Why are they not journeying?

KHIDR. I am *your* guide. I don't know why.
    But I will lead *you* there
    Though you resist.

20

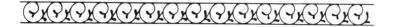

ALEXANDER.   I am not resisting!

KHIDR.   Then we must not look for reasons.
We are near. There is no need to explain.

ALEXANDER.   I want those whom I killed to live.

KHIDR.   I don't know where they are.
I know you.
Maybe when all the souls of conquerors . . .
Maybe when all the souls . . .
Are gathered together . . .
Maybe . . .
I am not wise. I can't complete the thought.

ALEXANDER.   You're wise. Just not intelligent.
In the worldly sense, I mean.
You haven't killed. You lack that sharpness
Of experience.

KHIDR.   We're going on. The stones are near.

ALEXANDER.   The dead are here to see if I will reach the well,
To see if I will put its water to my lips,
To see if I will dare to drink.

KHIDR.   We're near the site.

21

ALEXANDER.   Hephaestion is somewhere near.
    He never left my side in war.
    I want the manes and tails of horses cut.
    I want the "doctor" crucified
    Who failed to cure him of that rancid meat.
    My grief must be the world's!
    I warned them: Give up those soldiers
    You are hiding in your homes and temples.
    My soldiers warned repeatedly:
    There is no sanctuary!
    Would they listen? I had no choice.
    No one would trust my word if I backed down.
    I ordered no life left.
    I said: all life of theirs
    Is less in value than one of ours.
    That raised our pride.
    My men fought well
    Though small in number.
    You have to terrify to win.
    That was Persepolis.

KHIDR.   You left no life . . .

ALEXANDER.   I kept my Homer at my head.

KHIDR.   What of your friend, Patroclus?

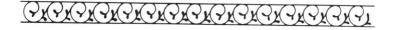

ALEXANDER.   A man does not live for friendship
   But for facing his mortality.
   I feel the smoke again
   In my lungs. Are we near
   The street of oil that burns
   In Babylon?

KHIDR.   No, closer to the sacred well.

ALEXANDER.   Your voice reminds me of another's,
   Of my teacher's, Aristotle's.
   It has his intonations,
   His subtle shifts in disposition.
   How I listened!
   I have never listened since
   To another voice
   As I did to his,
   Even to his silence,
   His deepest sighs,
   His strange hilarity
   Especially when he scoffed
   At talk of worlds to come.
   I hear his voice in yours.

KHIDR.   I have never been a teacher,
   Just a guide.

ALEXANDER. You've guided others?

KHIDR. Many.

ALEXANDER. Only to the sacred well?

KHIDR. Yes.

ALEXANDER. But your voice,
    It has his timbre.

KHIDR. You imagine resemblances.

ALEXANDER. Whom else did you guide?

KHIDR. No one important.

ALEXANDER. Have you credentials?

KHIDR. None. Except I know the way.

ALEXANDER. You ask me to trust you
    On resemblances alone?

KHIDR. No, on your own desire
    To reach the well.

24

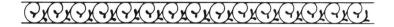

ALEXANDER.   Your voice is not the same.
I see that now.
Your voice is weak.
You speak in shorter sentences.
Yours lacks the worldliness of his,
The noble authority.
He held an audience enrapt
With choral odes from Sophocles
And the great hexameters of Homer.
Whom can you quote?

KHIDR.   You.
I can quote you on the world,
On pain, on power, on remorse;
But I may not be exact.

ALEXANDER.   Give me one quote. One.

KHIDR.   "Whom else did you guide?"

ALEXANDER.   Not nonsense like that,
Something remarkable,
A deeper thought.

KHIDR.   "Have you credentials?"

ALEXANDER.   I just asked you that.

KHIDR.   That's why I still remember it.

ALEXANDER.   I am disappearing from the world
In the presence of a fool
Who loiters on the outskirts of cities
Waiting for unsuspecting travelers
To take them to sacred wells that don't exist.

KHIDR.   Loitering is one of my favorite pastimes.

ALEXANDER.   I despise loitering
Or any waste of time.
The cities here are choked
With idleness.
With too many guides
And too little guidance.

KHIDR.   We are not far now.

ALEXANDER.   Not far. How can you tell?

KHIDR.   Some leave their tokens on the ground,
Pieces of silk, bits of stone,
Signs it has been visited.

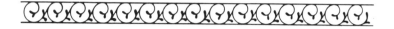

ALEXANDER.　Alone.
　　I want to visit it alone.

KHIDR.　You will be alone except for me.

ALEXANDER.　Will I cease to hear your voice
　　When we are there?
　　Will all my senses die?

KHIDR.　The senses change.

ALEXANDER.　You will keep speaking
　　Now that my eyes are blurred?

KHIDR.　Yes.

ALEXANDER.　There is a resemblance.
　　"Weak" is not the word.
　　Perhaps "intimate" is better
　　Or "less rhetorical,"
　　More "everyday."
　　You are not a speechmaker
　　But a quieter voice.
　　"Yes, I am your guide,"
　　You say as you stand idly
　　In the shadows of your archway

27

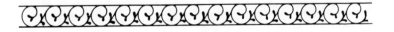

Where the stranger passes through.
Have you been with me long?

KHIDR.   Not long.

ALEXANDER.   Watching me long?

KHIDR.   No.

ALEXANDER.   You've seen me falter,
Show signs of needing help?

KHIDR.   No. I met you on the way
To the sacred well.
You asked me how far it was.
You asked me how it will be.

ALEXANDER.   Now I can barely see my hand
Before my eyes.

KHIDR.   We are almost there.

ALEXANDER.   Is there a bridge to cross?

KHIDR.   No.

ALEXANDER.   A raft to build?
I've learned in India

28

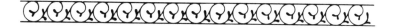

Men stand on rafts
To disappear
From their reality.

KHIDR.   No need for rafts. It is a well.

ALEXANDER.   There is no bridge,
No raft to build?

KHIDR.   The bridge was in your mind,
The raft was in another's.

ALEXANDER.   My metaphors for life,
My life, the world's life,
The only life I've known.
How can there be
No bridge to build, no sea to cross?

KHIDR.   I cup my hands
And hold the water to your lips.

ALEXANDER.   O Homer, help me now,
You are my soul,
You who have felt my pulse
And held my heart
Beating in your hands.
Khidr, I cannot drink.
I have seen my ruins.

KHIDR.   Monuments are lifeless. You must live.

ALEXANDER.   I cannot believe in guides, only in myself.

KHIDR.   The quest is for the flowing spring,
Not for guides.

ALEXANDER.   And it is here. But so is this last glimpse
Of ruins I have made.
The stares of the homeless, the old and maimed,
Are my perceptions now.
These ruins, and not the sacred well,
Make me immortal.
I know the world of monuments survives.

KHIDR.   There is a world beyond your monuments.

ALEXANDER.   Not in my mind. I see only what is in my mind.
I am afraid the journey was for nothing.

KHIDR.   Drink. It is cool and fresh.

ALEXANDER.   I cannot drink.
I feel the crumbling of my mind.

KHIDR.   It is the ruins dissolving.

ALEXANDER.   *I* am dissolving! I myself, all I have known.

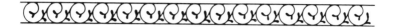

KHIDR.   Only the ruins. The selves we hold
 Are not our only selves.

ALEXANDER.   O Khidr, am I alone with death?

Khidr extends his hand to steady Alexander on his feet for this last encounter. The lights dim separating them, remaining a final moment on Alexander alone.

Spiritual Brotherhood:

A Note on the Source

In the tradition of Sufism there is a familiar allusion to mystics who, like Khidr, their archetypal guide, are forever conscious of one another ("two bodies but one soul") and carry in their waterbowls for each and others the water of life. *The Merchant and the Parrot* is an elaboration in dramatic form of this fraternal mystical theme.

The play is drawn from a Persian Sufi poem *Tuti va Bazargan* [The parrot and the merchant] by Rumi (d. 1273), written, then as now, on the subjects of self-enslavement and loss, spiritual brotherhood and substitution, transcendent love and freedom.

The Merchant
and the Parrot

Characters

in order of appearance

MARKET CROWD

ABULFULAN THE MERCHANT

HIS HOME ENTOURAGE

AHMAD THE EUNUCH

TWO POETS

ZUMURRAD

THE PARROT

CARAVAN MASTER

AND ENTOURAGE

AN OLD POET

SHETH

A PARROT

PART ONE

Before us is a large Persian miniature with careful detail of people, birds, animals, flowers, all in rich color tones of blue, red, gold, and green. It lifts to a scrim and closer detail of a marketplace and a bridge of boats. The scene is busy with merchants and customers, passersby, children, beggars, monkeys, et al. An overweight, overdressed merchant, Abulfulan, rings his little bell, doles money out generously while calling attention to himself. He shows a gradual fatigue, steps forward, apart, the ringing stops.

ABULFULAN.   Enough! I have fulfilled the tax.
My mood has changed.
All the caresses of the market now offend me,
No, disgust me. I must bathe. God, I loathe
To be pawed, fondled, fingered, yes, that too.
The poor are an abomination and a bore.
They only want want want and wait on chance
Indulgences. I can't abide incessant
Supplication. I've been too good,
Too decent, too open to humanity.
Twelve gold pieces was a mite too much.
But still I was observed. The qadi heard my bell—
His silk was too rich for a judge. Ha!
I hate dishonesty in judges, hypocrisy in scribes.
I hate our times:
The violence, the noise, the arrogance of experts,
Technological advance. The waterclocks speed life

39

Too fast, the astrolabe brings stars too near,
The naptha bombs strip war of manliness,
The mystery of God Himself is next to go.
Our young are rude, our women willful—
The two presages of social dissolution.
There is no quiet, no peace, no love, no trust. Ah!
I want my home, my peace, my hideaway from all of this.
Here, let me through.
Praise be to—yes,—Praise be—yes, God is great.
Let me through. I've done enough for humankind today. Yes.
It's past dusk.—God is—yes—oh, let me through!
Indeed, our God is great!

*Suddenly he is within his own walls. He shuts the doors be-
hind him to close out the noisy, intrusive world. Servants
come, followed by wives, children, poets, and other beseech-
ers: a new crowd within his own walls. He is already ex-
hausted, announces:*

One by one please. I must bathe and pray.
I will receive each of you one at a time. Please,
Don't speak now. Oh, how I hate children.
I must be alone, except for Ahmad my servant—
Where is that shiftless Zanj?

*Ahmad, a black eunuch dressed in richly embroidered silk
robes, elegant in style, steps forward to attend his master.*

They are alone in the privacy of an inner chamber. A bath is
prepared.

ABULFULAN.   Ahmad, you poor unmanned bastard, speak to me
    Soothingly with wit and style. At least I know
    What you have no capacity to do to me and mine.

> *Ahmad removes the merchant's clothes, behind a*
> *half screen, down to the gold key around his neck*
> *as he descends into bath.*

No, not that. You know no one can take that from me
Ever—no one. I alone can touch that. I *alone.*

> *He hits Ahmad on the face, then shows chagrin in*
> *his expression.*

That was *too* hard. I'm sorry I had to strike you.
Now you make me feel bad by your transgression.
I hate the moral pain of cruelty you make me use.
Can't you understand, I am the humanity by which
You're measured here. Try to learn that one fact.

AHMAD.   I'm sorry I presumed, Abulfulan.
    You know I meant no harm.
    I'm sorry that I am no true servant,
    For enough was left to me to still presume.
    I wish I could be perfect, master,

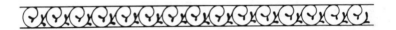

Do your bidding, ask no favors,
Facilitate my master to bestow his favors
As he wishes, not expecting, not imposing,
Being as if invisible, nonexistent,
Like God's servants when they're truly His
With no particle of self retained except His self.
Oh, God is great, and you are great, master,
And I am a humble and inadequate servant
Who cannot even serve selflessly without offending.

ABULFULAN.   You have been listening to our street mystics.

AHMAD.   No, master, only to my own heart's desire.

ABULFULAN.   Nonsense, you go among them.
I have seen you in the crowd.

AHMAD.   No, master, no; I listen only to you,
Not to them.

ABULFULAN.   Liar.

AHMAD.   No.

ABULFULAN.   I said liar.

AHMAD.   All right, if it's God's will—liar.

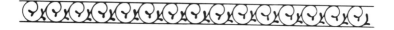

ABULFULAN. See, you are too humble to be true.
No one is so humble without a motive.

AHMAD. I have no motive but to serve.

ABULFULAN. No one has no motive but to serve. Liar, liar.
I know the world.

AHMAD. Go on, master, call me a liar if it gives you peace.

ABULFULAN. Stop that. It gives no peace, damn your black
hide.
Our teachers of religion pervert you poor bastards
When they work you through to your conversions.
Can't you see, they made you feel the highest thing
There is to serve is God unquestioningly, and me
As His khalifa in your heart. Can't you see,
I want the truth, not abject humanity I can't believe.
Be something of yourself, a man, at least that much.

AHMAD. Well, I have attended sermons once or twice
Down by the Tigris south of the Khalif's tower.
One spoke of freeing blacks and ending the atrocious
Practise of making eunuchs—

ABULFULAN. That's too much!
Just be truthful, not subversive.

AHMAD.   Yes, master. I believe the practise should be kept,
    Atrocious as it is.

ABULFULAN.   Enough! No irony, just truth.

AHMAD.   Yes, master. You have body odor, master.

ABULFULAN.   Stop! Go back to lying and deception.
    God, you can't find decent servants anymore!

AHMAD.   I'm only here to serve.

ABULFULAN.   Shut up! Get me out of this.

Ahmad holds the towels.

AHMAD.   The poets are here, master.

ABULFULAN.   Poets? What do *they* want?

AHMAD.   To sponge your soul
    Once I have dried your body.

ABULFULAN.   Are they never satisfied?

AHMAD.   It gives them pleasure to praise.
    Your person is remarkable,

44

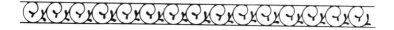

The body of mankind himself,
The model which all admire,
The metaphor for all of us.

ABULFULAN.   All?

AHMAD.   All who have their senses still about them.

ABULFULAN.   All but you, you mean.

AHMAD.   I have retained enough to know your glories as a
    man.

ABULFULAN.   Adroitly said.
    You do well as you are.
    I'll see the poets, tedious as they can be.
    No, don't dry the key. Gold dries itself, this gold.
    I'll see them in my outer chamber.
    Tell Zumurrad not to leave me too long with them.
    Just long enough for condiments, not dessert.
    She'll understand. Tell her precisely: not dessert.

AHMAD.   I understand you, master,
    Though I am a eunuch.

ABULFULAN.   Now go and let the sponges of my soul come in.
    How many are there waiting with their drying verses?

AHMAD. Two.

ABULFULAN. Only two?

AHMAD. I drove the other twelve away
　　Believing you were tired.
　　I am sure I chose the best.

ABULFULAN. Very clever of you. Let's hope you did.

The stage darkens and when light returns the colors are bold and lush. A receiving room for indulgences. Large deep pillows, bold greens, golds, reds, elaborate brocade, a huge oriental carpet with smaller adjacent carpets prayer-size, hanging lamps, wall tiles turquoise and white, subtle lighting, sensuous aura. Ahmad stands like a statue to one side observing as two rather modestly dressed poets bow and scrape before Abulfulan, who sits centrally above, elevated on his pillows, regally dressed as their host and potential benefactor in his flowing Hindustani silks.

AHMAD. Be seated, one on each side of my master;
　　No, slightly further back [*i.e., down to stage front*],
　　Lean lower; that's it. Now, you sir.

ABULFULAN. You mustn't mind my servant. He is brusque,
　　But only moderately less than I myself

When tested as to patience.
[*The poets cringe noticeably.*]
Now what do you do, or should I say
How well do you compose ex tempore, and for how much?
[*They stammer in protest simultaneously, then Poet One
    speaks.*]

POET ONE.   We come to celebrate a reputation we have heard
    abroad.

ABULFULAN.   How well can you celebrate what now at last
    you've seen?

POET TWO.   An instant is a total confirmation
    Of one whose outer form and inner substance are as one.

AHMAD.   Good, that's good. A rhyme cannot be wholly wrong
    Even if the latter hemistich is overlong.

> *The poets look over their shoulders nervously at
> Ahmad.*

ABULFULAN.   Why do our poets these days have to think
    Of *substances* instead of entertain with sounds
    And sights of beauty and the joy of life?
    I long for the old sweet melancholy odes,

The exploits of the Badu both in love and war.
They were the lovers of the world. The way they grasped
A woman's thighs in both their hands and hardened
To the deepening dark waters of her inmost soul.
Those men could draw their swords and kill for love.

AHMAD [*to the poets*].   Can you both recreate that mood for
     him?
He likes to hear the sound of steel on steel.

POET ONE.   The times have changed. The Badu have been out
     Of fashion in this city for years. . . .

ABULFULAN.   What!

AHMAD.   Erase that thought.

POET TWO.   I could try. I think they're coming back.

ABULFULAN.   You have the balls at least to try.
     I'll listen then to you, not to your fat friend.

POET TWO [*tentative*].   In olden times, when men clashed
     with their swords
To settle issues that we now resolve with words—

ABULFULAN.   In "olden times"? No, *now*—still!

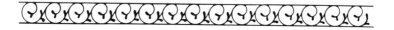

POET TWO.   In these times, *still*, when men upraise their swords
   And put to rout all slothful silly limpish words . . .

ABULFULAN.   Good, good . . .

AHMAD.   At least, better.

POET TWO.   And women had such deep dark watery eyes
   As fleet gazelles or eagles soaring through the skies —

ABULFULAN.   *Had* such eyes, had?

POET TWO.   And women *have* far deeper darker eyes
   Than any creatures of the seas or skies.
   Oh, then, yes, then
   No spindly legged men

ABULFULAN.   No, now, now.

POET TWO.   Oh, now to feel the looseness of their thighs
   When I swim forth in darkness through the skies —

ABULFULAN.   Looseness — swim — my God!
   Can't anyone write poetry anymore?

POET TWO.   Looseness of the sheath, tightness of the thighs
   Makes a man's sword gleam forth and rise.

49

ABULFULAN. That's terrible!

Tell me, poet, do you know either women or war?

POET TWO. I try to please, the best that I can do.

ABULFULAN. How can you please if you know nothing of what
please me?

Give me a poem of what *you* know best and I'll give you

What I think the effort's worth. But it must be sponta-
neous

And strong, not learned and weak, or God's glaive upon
your necks.

POET TWO. I do literary criticism best.

ABULFULAN. What's that?

POET ONE. I do commentary on the world best.

ABULFULAN. What commentary, what world?

POET ONE. This world, the world of power in high places.

ABULFULAN. A theoretical poet.

POET TWO. I do images of self, too.

ABULFULAN. A Narcissist. The Greeks *have* poisoned us!

AHMAD.   And made us all believe we can teach.

ABULFULAN.   You're right, my Ahmad.
   The age is filled with poets who think they're benefactors.

AHMAD [*sotto voce*].   And benefactors who think they're poets.

ABULFULAN.   You should sing the old songs,
   Learn the old poems.
   There is nothing new to equal them.
   A poet is a praiser—yes?—of life.

AHMAD.   And my master is your metaphor for life.

POET ONE.   I'll make an ode in monorhyme to *you* as life.

POET TWO.   And I'll attempt to sheath the lover's knife.

ABULFULAN.   Sword, sword, not merely knife;
   Unsheath, not sheath. Don't you know the difference?

AHMAD.   They know, they know.

POETS.   We do? we do?

ABULFULAN.   Then do, then do.

Silence of anticipation.

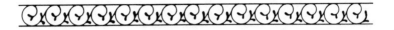

POET ONE.   The world is but a hemistich of verse . . .

POET TWO.   The thighs of war are tightening or worse . . .

ABULFULAN.   Oh, God.

Suddenly an extraordinary beauty, Zumurrad, enters dancing, all in silk, emerald, veiled. Abulfulan waves his hands violently. Ahmad drives the poets away after the master throws them each a few gold coins pulled from his fat waist clumsily and curses them roundly.

POETS.   We only tried to please . . .

AHMAD.   And now move backward on your knees.

They run in disarray.

ABULFULAN [*to Ahmad*].   Leave us.
    I want no interruption now. You understand?

AHMAD.   Of course, my lord and master, he who knows
    The thighs of war and love, his passion glows.

ABULFULAN.   Stop. God, stop this rhyming and get out. [*He throws his fists at him in lieu of objects, then finds slipper and hurls it. Ahmad runs chanting:*]

AHMAD.   *Still* the coals of the deserted campfire glow;
The camel's buttocks heave and sigh, oh oh, oh oh.

ABULFULAN [*throws other slipper at him, strains back, cries out
in pain*]:   Ow!

*Ahmad leaves. Abulfulan rises awkwardly and begins to
chase Zumurrad around the stage. She drops a veil each time
he touches her. The chase ends with his being breathless and
her withholding further charms.*

ZUMURRAD.   Oh, my lover, have you strained your back again?
[*She rubs his back gently.*]

ABULFULAN.   That is good, better, better still.
How much better do your hands soothe
Than do any poet's words.

ZUMURRAD.   Why do you beat your servant so?

ABULFULAN.   He brought me two inane poets
To sponge my soul. They only scratched my ass
With their mediocre wits.

ZUMURRAD.   [*Laughs naughtily.*]
But you should beat them, not him;
He's only black and hasn't anything to blame.

ABULFULAN.　But if I beat them, they would want to be
　　My servants. Sponges are like that.

ZUMURRAD.　My poor Abulfulan, your life is much beset
　　With all kinds of demands and hardships.
　　Was the day completely without reward?

ABULFULAN.　The day had its rewards. The night will now have
　　its.

ZUMURRAD.　Of course.

ABULFULAN.　Today my workers poured 1,000 glass containers
　　full.
　　Imagine that!

ZUMURRAD.　That is amazing. Is it true the naphtha that they
　　pour
　　Can burn the skin right off a man?

ABULFULAN.　In war my glasses are efficient.
　　I do not like to imagine it
　　But we must be strong against our enemies.
　　Preparedness is everything.

ZUMURRAD.　I thought love was everything.

ABULFULAN.   Exactly.
We guarantee security only so that we can love.

ZUMURRAD.   You do too much for the Community and not
enough for yourself.

ABULFULAN.   A man of my possessions has responsibilities.

ZUMURRAD.   And everyone admires you.

ABULFULAN.   That's too strong a word.

ZUMURRAD.   No, too weak a word. *Adores* you, seeks you out
for praise.

ABULFULAN.   You think so?

ZUMURRAD.   Ahmad tells me so.

ABULFULAN.   Ahmad! Perhaps he's not a liar after all.

ZUMURRAD.   No, he's devoted despite his being what he is.

ABULFULAN.   Why are we talking about him?

ZUMURRAD.   I feel sad. That's why I'm talking nonsense,
To avoid the subject burning in my heart.

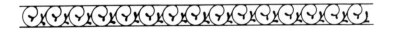

ABULFULAN.   Yes, I know. Already you are missing me.

ZUMURRAD.   You know. You are so sensitive
   To others' weaknesses of body, mind, and heart.

ABULFULAN.   It's already Thursday, my beloved jewel;
   But we must not anticipate.
   It wastes the time we have.

ZUMURRAD.   But I'm consumed with loneliness
   In my anticipation now. Help me to know
   How to endure the next two days
   And then the lonely weeks ahead
   When you are far away in Hindustan.

ABULFULAN.   I love your loneliness for me.
   You ask me anything, anything at all.
   If we must be sad, then tell me, love,
   What you most want me to bring you as a gift:
   A robe of Indian silk, a jewel, anything.
   I love your sad deep darkening eyes.

ZUMURRAD.   You are so loving, my lord.

ABULFULAN.   I love the murmur of your voice,
   Like the echo of a mournful nightingale.

ZUMURRAD.   I'd like a jewel, a large green jewel,
An emerald, the largest in the world.

ABULFULAN.   For your navel. Ah!

ZUMURRAD.   For yourself. I know what pleases my host
Reflects his generosity the most.

ABULFULAN.   I love you, my true poet, as no other jewel,
My emerald, my love.

ZUMURRAD.   And I you, Abulfulan.
The jewel is only a glimmer of your kindness.

ABULFULAN.   You shall have it.
If I have to give all my wealth and weaponry away
To our enemies to get it, it shall be yours.
Now, what have you for me?

ZUMURRAD.   [*She smiles and lifts the veils from her bosom.
She then flits away.*]
Not here — not yet — my love —
Not everything — some things are mysteries
Hidden in another room, an inner room.

ABULFULAN.   Like the darkening purple of an orchid
As one approaches with the eye the inner depths

57

Within the petals, petal by petal,
Like two lips separating . . .

ZUMURRAD.   My lips, my lord, are yours. [*She leaves.*]

ABULFULAN.   Ohhh! I will find your inner room—soon.

                              Ahmad returns.

AHMAD.   Did things go smoothly or, indeed, *well*, master?

ABULFULAN.   Flowingly, flowingly.

AHMAD.   Ah, nothing happened yet.

ABULFULAN.   What? Of course it did. I said it did.

AHMAD.   I see.

ABULFULAN.   Things move in stages, don't you know?

AHMAD.   No, I don't. How could I? You know my state.

ABULFULAN.   Of course, you don't; I'm telling you.

AHMAD.   You're telling me what you *achieved*.

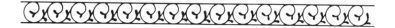

ABULFULAN.   You don't use words like that in love.

AHMAD.   What words do you use — coitus unfulfilledus?

ABULFULAN.   No, no! I told you, don't use foreign words in this house.

AHMAD.   My lips, like hers, are sealed.

ABULFULAN.   You are disgusting — no, vulgar, at the very least.

AHMAD.   Curtailed vulgarity is always disgusting.
Vulgarity freed is sweet.

ABULFULAN.   If you knew love, you would not be clever at a time like this.
Love calls for lightness, silences, brushes of the hand
Against the face, a word of sweet appreciation
In appreciation of sweetness, the promise of a future gift,
A hope of something more than melancholy loss or fate,
A delicate maneuver that you let her think she makes,
A whisper to suggest she is doing, not just *well*, but perfectly,
A whisper that brings you to the edge of saying "love"
And makes her listen to the silence anxiously, quiveringly,

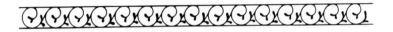

With her own yearning for the word, and then you touch
    her
Softly, gently, and fill the silence with yourself.

AHMAD.   You filled the silence now, not then.

ABULFULAN.   You were watching from the lattice wings.
    I've told you not to watch.

AHMAD.   But it's the favorite pastime of the impotent, master.

ABULFULAN.   I know nothing of impotence.

AHMAD.   Of course, you don't—and I'm not being clever
    Or metaphorical (the favorite art of impotence)—
    As you are a wise merchant and understand
    How boring cleverness and metaphor can be;
    And boredom (the greatest fear of impotence)
    Is a thing you shouldn't have to bear;
    You much prefer religion (the purest science of impotence).

ABULFULAN.   Don't speak against religion in my presence.
    I've warned you about that.

AHMAD.   I've gone too far.
    Let me retract (the constant task of impotence).

You much prefer your time alone with guileless Zumurrad
(The favorite fantasy of impotence!)

ABULFULAN.   Now stop. I've heard enough.

AHMAD.   But you are not an impotent, as you well know,
Even though your world may be the spawning ground
Of impotents, as well as of progenitors.
Your place is safe among the powerful
Who know themselves, who fondle what they have,
And need not mourn their losses constantly and sigh
To God, the Potent One, the Powerful, in vain.

ABULFULAN.   What are you talking about?

AHMAD.   The freedom from fear virility enjoys.

ABULFULAN.   Yes, of course.
It's fearful to think of being impotent.

AHMAD.   Especially when there's still so much to lose.

ABULFULAN.   I think you're being clever.
But no matter, I'm barely listening.
I see Zumurrad's—no, I taste Zumurrad's
Lips upon my lips.

AHMAD.   And your appetite is whetted for more.

ABULFULAN.   You understand.

AHMAD.   I don't know how
With my limitations.

ABULFULAN.   Understanding is in the mind
Not in the balls, man.

AHMAD.   You called me "man."
"Not in the balls, man," you said.

ABULFULAN.   It was a figure of speech, nothing more.
We both know you are not a man.

AHMAD.   I might've been. I even was once.

ABULFULAN.   Perhaps it's not completely hopeless to be
impotent,
Only disappointing.

AHMAD.   And a eunuch, unlike others, can be measured
For excellence
By the way he reconciles himself to disappointment.

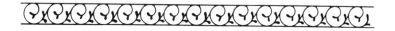

ABULFULAN.   Exactly.

AHMAD.   Were you ever disappointed?

ABULFULAN.   I was never impotent.

AHMAD.   Then how can you understand?

ABULFULAN.   Hush. I am tired of cleverness.
I want to be alone
You know with whom
And where I'll be [*he fondles the gold key at his neck*],
And there I will not be disturbed
Or watched.

AHMAD.   I know. I know.
I'll leave you alone
And serve you only when you call.
Your bell is always heard
And never left unanswered.
That is the grace of the truly impotent.
May God grant you your desires
And continue you in your prosperity
And my poor altered self in your beneficence.

ABULFULAN.   Amen. Now go!

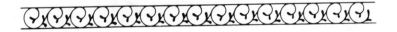

*Ahmad the servant withdraws. The mood of Abulfulan
changes, deepens. Interlude music is very quiet, two instru-
ments—oud and reed pipe—in lyric Bird Theme repeated as
appropriate to the end. Curtains withdraw to reveal an inner
chamber, the inmost heart itself, the private sanctuary which
only he enters. Suddenly, by his pulling of a final curtain, there
is revealed an extraordinary varicolored bird, a tuti, a talking
bird, in a golden cage: referred to as both a parrot and a night-
ingale. The cage and bird are very large, hyperbolized from
Abulfulan's adoring point of view. We see the bird as a person
with feathered arms, etc., beautifully plumaged. Either a man
or a woman could play the part, but in either case without any
sexual overtones or sensual mannerisms and intonations. The
bird blends its voice with the two instruments at times to the
end.*

ABULFULAN.   I have been counting the seconds until I could be
   alone with you again.

BIRD.   The seconds . . . alone . . . again . . .

ABULFULAN.   Yes, alone with you again . . . your voice, your
   transcendent colors, your presence, your otherworldly wis-
   dom, your self.

BIRD.   Your self . . . alone with your self . . .

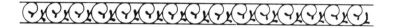

ABULFULAN. No, *your* self.

I am tired, as always, of my self. Day after day I face the world. It is the same, I am the same. I crave some other self. Only you understand, only you provide that other self I crave—by your voice, your beauty, your . . .

BIRD. Self I crave . . .

ABULFULAN. Yes, yes. You understand perfectly, as always.

BIRD. As always. I understand perfectly, though I only echo you.

ABULFULAN. What?

BIRD. What?

ABULFULAN. Yes, that's better. I thought you said something else.

BIRD. Something else . . . than what I thought you said. You want to hear yourself as something else than what you are.

ABULFULAN. I love your riddles, but I want to hear your singing voice, your sweet sad lyric voice.

65

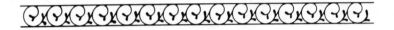

BIRD.   Your sweet sad lyric voice . . . you crave to hear your-
self in echo endlessly . . .

> *The oud and reed pipe are heard quietly again as*
> *the bird begins to sing.*

ABULFULAN [*interrupts*].   No, your self, not my self. I am
tired of my self.

BIRD.   You're tired of your self, so tired, tired of your self, and
yet you only want an echo of yourself. That's why you're
tired. You listen to yourself and are so tired of your self. You
are just one old tired self so tired of yourself repeatedly.

ABULFULAN.   That's not the sweet sad song I thought I'd hear.
I want to hear your melody.

BIRD.   Yourself, yourself, your tired self is sweet and sad and
tiresome to hear.

ABULFULAN.   Yes, but not your self. You are not tiresome to
hear. If you would only sing that other self's sweet lyric
song I love to hear.

BIRD.   Which song? I am an echo of yourself which you have
caged. I have no other song to sing but songs of being caged

to sing you songs of your old tired self that longs to hear
some other song but can't because you have that key around
your neck to keep me caged so I will sing the sweet sad song
of your old tired self that can't escape your self because you
cage your self and are afraid if you release the echo bird
you'll lose your self.

ABULFULAN.   Now you repeat yourself. You're sounding like
the world. I expected something different in my inmost
heart.

BIRD.   Different like the world expecting something other
than itself it cages endlessly. The key is there around your
neck against your heart. Your fingers hold it.

ABULFULAN.   A song, a song! I came for peace, not more frus-
tration and reason to be angry. I am tired of the world.

BIRD.   Or tired of yourself and angry with the world. A song.
A song! A sweet sad song, of brothers who once lived to-
gether in the trees and the tall grass of Khuhistan, who
vowed to love as brothers love, to send each other mes-
sages with deeds not words or only simple words that could
release. This brother waits here for a brother's word. . .

ABULFULAN.   What are you talking about?

67

BIRD. . . . for his release.

ABULFULAN. I feed you.

BIRD. This brother longs for his release.

ABULFULAN. But why? I treat you well. The others would destroy you out of ignorance or jealousy if they could get their vulgar hands on this key. This key is your salvation, believe me, *brother!*

BIRD. I believe you, brother.

ABULFULAN. I understand you. I appreciate you.

BIRD. Appreciate and understand.

ABULFULAN. The world is mad and dangerous with all this talk about release, release.

BIRD. Now you repeat yourself, like me yourself.

ABULFULAN. I love you, I worship you, I protect you.

BIRD. From my self.

ABULFULAN. From the world, from others.

BIRD. My brothers, in the trees and fields of tall grass in Khuhistan, send me your word . . . your word . . . word.

ABULFULAN. Lonely. That was your lonely melody, just then. I love it when you sing your sweet sad lonely melody I know so well. I would never abandon you to others, to the world.

BIRD. Appreciate and understand, there might be songs you've never heard that I could sing if I were free.

ABULFULAN. I love the sweet sad songs you sing.

BIRD. I talk too much.

ABULFULAN. Now you're your self, when you can mock yourself. Now sing, no talk, just sing.

BIRD. I sing of life inside my cage, my golden cage,
Of radiant green and red and yellow plumage . . .

ABULFULAN. Sing on, yes, more like that.

BIRD. But I don't want to sing or to be radiant for your possession. These things are of no importance to true friends.

ABULFULAN. But they show us in a light that makes us worthy of creation.

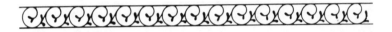

BIRD.   We are of creation. We don't need cages to make us worthy.

ABULFULAN.   That's all right for you, but have pity on me who lacks your gifts. Hearing you gives me light and lifts my sad day of being just a merchant of destruction. I too hate the world's curse upon us.

BIRD.   Why don't you flee the world, no one has you in a cage?

ABULFULAN.   You don't see it, but someone has a key around his neck and keeps me doing what I do. I would rather be a singer of sad tales. The same one who created you so beautiful created me fat and ugly and holds a key around his neck so I would find you in an open field and capture you to sing for me. Without you in my life, my life would be without release. We are bound together. It is not my fault.

BIRD.   You reason strangely and you think I'm strange.
I could appreciate and risk a sweet exchange
Of our positions. I would never make you sing
But send you to your brothers never wanting anything.
The silence could be beautiful and you could teach
The sweetness of your human heart to reach
Without possessiveness a vision with your eye,
And I could rediscover what a simple thing it is to fly.

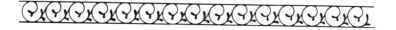

ABULFULAN. You enjoy here with me your own simplicity. You don't need to experience to know you are a bird.

BIRD. I don't need to know, I only need to be.

ABULFULAN. Now you are too obscure. You think too much, like Ahmad.

BIRD. You give me too much luxury of imprisonment.

ABULFULAN. You are never satisfied.

BIRD. Oh yes, I could be, simply.

ABULFULAN. I hear the world around me wanting everything.

BIRD. You hear the echoing voice you cage inside your heart.

ABULFULAN. I crave beauty—is that wrong!

BIRD. Let me tell a little story too simple for any man's but not a bird's intelligence. It is a story of two flowers that lived near the shadows of a woods beside a clearing. They thought they were Narcissuses, which draw to shade as roses draw to light; until one day the light attracted them to itself and they saw each other instead of only their selves, and they discovered they were not those flowers

71

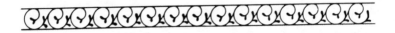

that leaned only to shade. Suddenly they did not close again in contemplation of themselves, but burst open to the light, discovering they were roses.

It may be you have only thought you are a Narcissus because you have concealed your heart in shade.

ABULFULAN.   I prefer you to lament your fate than to teach me mine.

The music ceases. They stare in silence at each other a few moments, then Abulfulan speaks softly, compassionately:

ABULFULAN.   I am setting out soon on caravan through Khuhistan to Hindustan. It is that time for me again. No one will harm you, I promise, or I'll have their livers. As long as they know that and are afraid, both of us are safe. I trust no one and nothing but myself and this key. [*Fondles it continually.*] I want you to be happy. I want you to think hard what you would like me to bring you from my journey—any gift at all. I will ask you to tell me what it is before I leave. I want you above all others to have what you wish.

He draws the curtain over the cage and he is alone again as the lights slowly dim.

INTERLUDE

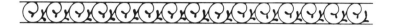

AHMAD THE SERVANT [*alone*]:   Eavesdropping—the lot of the truly impotent. But now I'll let him be. Even I derive no pleasure from what he's doing *now*. The man congratulates himself with every exercise of nature, whereas I find my remaining functions merely a matter of course, like the flowing prose I was educated in when I was rendered impotent, when I was brought in from the jungle, so to speak, and separated from my manhood by the glaive as were my boyhood friends, transported by a single stroke, or sometimes two it took, of a jagged blade, into the articulate and wealthy and castrating world—here to serve, to eavesdrop, to be an echo to my master, who is amused by what I say: in sum, to be removed forever from creativeness, to live among onlookers, vicarious experiencers, theatregoers. I've seen a lot of people powerless right here who never felt the blade. But then that is also the lot of the truly impotent—ironic detachment. Some of my friends and brothers did better than I: they rose in the military, became officials of the state, served as agents of more powerful merchants than Abulfulan, became wealthy in their own right as scribes, bankers, lawyers, patrons of the arts, dispensers of others' wealth, but even then they only drew close to power; they never became powerful themselves. They only echoed at a higher level, became copies of greater scoundrels, sometimes holding the sword handle, never the sword. Of course, the impotent enjoys a

powerful man's waving of what he doesn't have himself to wave. On the other hand, the impotent escapes the pro-scriptions of religion and the law, except for murder and the like, by being weak by definition. I am a category—slave, and therefore less responsible and of no moral con-sequence, protected, tolerated, like minorities of faiths. The masters, on the other hand, attract the scuttling feet of many mice who come to take a further bite out of their great cheese. At least I am free of all of that. But then, again, to think I'm free of anything is an illusion of the impotent, for what is freedom if it is defined only by an experience I cannot have? Of course, I have the experience of thinking about the meaning of freedom—another of the impotent's major preoccupations: to reduce to ab-straction what is only meaningful in experience. The prob-lem of separation from reality never leaves one when one is torn from the romanticized jungle of one's childhood. It is sad that one loses innocence by exposure to the world of men, but that one is made impotent only to serve the power of those men as they grow older, fatter, less secure about themselves—is grotesque!

This impotence, I've seen, takes many forms. I am only the lowest kind, the actual impotent, the legally ac-cepted in this anachronistic world, the basis of all the metaphors. The other forms are my unrealized offspring. I am their progenitor. As long as I persist anywhere in the

world the others will be because of me. But that, too, though intriguing as a truth of sorts, is an illusion of the impotent—that he creates at all. He *sees,* he does indeed *see,* and that may help others recognize themselves in him, but it cannot help himself. Like words themselves, I know I am only of passing interest to anyone—even here —alas!

PART TWO

Commotion of the merchant's preparations for departure: Wives, numerous children each more or less huddled around each wife separately, with a few smaller ones straying together, playing; minor servants being officious; luggage heaped; a katib (scribe) with a writing table set up accounting all the goods being taken; a caravan leader impatiently waiting to depart; a treasurer; an old poet, not one of the previous beseechers, companion of the way, stands apart as if viewing the whole.

The merchant enters with Ahmad. He is even more overdressed than before, and overprepared to satisfy his needs on the journey. He is frustrated even as he is gratified by what he sees.

ABULFULAN.   My God, all these are mine, and all of them want something.

AHMAD.   It's your generosity, master. You have spoiled them all, they expect gratuity from you.

ABULFULAN.   I don't know them. Where is Zumurrad? and where is my nightingale?

AHMAD.   It would not do for them to be here. You'll see them privately in a moment.

ABULFULAN.   Help me get through this business and I'll reward you handsomely.

AHMAD. How could you reward me as I wish to be rewarded?

ABULFULAN. Name your highest gratuity.

AHMAD. Must I in public? [*sighs, laughs*] I'll help you through this. I ask no gift of the impossible.

ABULFULAN. Who is that? He's too old to be a son of mine.

AHMAD. He's your caravan poet. You asked for one to sing you songs reminding you of home.

ABULFULAN. God, he's ugly. Couldn't you have arranged for someone of more felicitous appearance to call my home to mind?

AHMAD. Home is one's own ageing in nostalgia as its poets age in beauty, my master.

ABULFULAN. I would like someone younger, handsomer, to remind me of myself as I once was.

AHMAD. It's too late to find one. There's no cause to be agitated about something as inconsequential as one's loss of illusions about oneself.

ABULFULAN. That sounds ominously wise. Can we move on?

He stops at one veiled woman surrounded by
children.

AHMAD.   Your third wife, master.

ABULFULAN.   Yes, of course. I know my third wife—I think.
And what would you and my children—all four [*counts*],
five of you—like me to bring you from Hindustan?

No one speaks; giggles.

Come on, speak. Your shyness dims my generosity in the
world's eyes.

AHMAD.   Toys that work by winding, master. I think they're
saying: mechanical toys.

CHILDREN.   Yes, yes, yes, yes. Toys that wind.

ABULFULAN.   Toys that wind. And how about a monkey or an
elephant or a snake, a big long snake to charm with a reed
pipe?

CHILDREN.   No. Toys that wind! We don't want real animals.

ABULFULAN.   My God. They're all addicted to machines. Is
there no feeling for nature left in the young. I used to—

AHMAD. An old complaint, master.

ABULFULAN. Must you prod me with that word—*old?*

AHMAD. The women want new silk robes, perfumes, jewelry . . .

ABULFULAN. What would I do without a eunuch to read my women's minds?

AHMAD. I hate to think.

> *The merchant looks up and sees Zumurrad in a window standing in a green silk jalaba and head veil. She doesn't speak or call.*

ABULFULAN. Yes, yes, I remember, my love . . . Zumurrad, my emerald.

> *He savors her appearance, then she leaves the window. He turns to Ahmad.*

I know what she desires.

> *Ahmad is silent, head bowed.*

I'll find something to surprise you with.

AHMAD [*joking*]. Did your nightingale ask you for a gift?

ABULFULAN. You know better than to laugh about that.
[*Fondles key.*] Yes, we have spoken together privately.
It is our secret.
You will see that he is fed and cared for.
You know he likes a little sweet . . .

AHMAD. You like to think he likes a little sweet.

ABULFULAN. You care for him as I say.

AHMAD. Or the glaive will strike my neck!

ABULFULAN. [*He stares threateningly.*] Exactly.
Nothing means as much to me as my precious night-
    ingale,
Nothing!

> *The oud and reed pipe repeat the Bird's Theme as*
> *the illusion of the caged bird is shown.*

BIRD. When you see my brothers free in the meadows and
    the trees,
Tell them a brother sits here in a cage yearning to be free.

> *The merchant and his entourage leave for the*
> *journey as Ahmad is left alone before the image of*
> *the cage; he covers it perfunctorily by a gesture*
> *with its gold silk cover.*

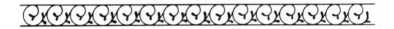

Somewhere on the caravan route, Abulfulan
shadowed by the old poet.

POET.   The air is dry, the wind is still, the grass is motionless.
The smell of beggars greets the nose, the dissonance of
foreign tongues the ears.
Nothing recalls the luxury of home as the foul water of
foreign wells.

ABULFULAN.   You are like a poet, not like my nightingale.

POET.   The precious bird that summons the soul to home.

ABULFULAN.   Isn't it premature to sing of home just one day
out?

POET.   The hardest pain is that which follows on the feet
Of separation. It is sharp and quick like the cut of a knife,
And then the painful healing starts . . .

ABULFULAN.   Do I want the healing to start?

POET.   You miss your favorite, Zumurrad.

ABULFULAN.   I miss my singing bird I have left at home.

POET.   The sweetest love is that reborn by loss.

ABULFULAN.   By loss? [*He is anxious.*]

POET.   Of home, not of your singing bird.
    I spoke in figures not in facts.
    The sweetest love is love one thinks is lost
    And in despair finds stowed away inside the heart.
    He least expects what he most yearns to find.
    A merchant counts his wares
    Yet never lists his secret room of loss;
    This room is occupied by Night
    Who answers lovers cries. A merchant has a soul
    Forever fitted out for journeys in the dark
    To bring to memory what it seeks of light.
    A merchant cannot live by words alone—

ABULFULAN.   Enough—for now.
    It was good. I thank you. But you make me think.
    I need to journey for awhile, not think. You understand?

POET.   A poet's is a soul of words not thoughts.
    He might sing on and on but for imperatives like "think!"

ABULFULAN.   The truth is I hate traveling, despise the
    inconveniences,
    Have no desire for new experiences, hate foreignness in
    food,

Have no ear for others' languages, the toiletries of strangers
Jar my nerves, I constipate for days . . .

POET.   Poor merchant soul—despises travel
Yet must always seek new treasures from abroad.

ABULFULAN.   By customer demand.

POET.   New treasures to justify the weapons you create.

ABULFULAN.   To protect our way of life from foreigners.

POET.   Two lines of merchandise.

ABULFULAN.   One must diversify to stay alive.

POET.   And must keep caged the sorrow of this paradox.

ABULFULAN.   What?

POET.   A poet's play of words.
Sometimes another finds a meaning I cannot,
Which is the cagèd sorrow of *my* paradox.

ABULFULAN.   You are a true companion of my fears.
But now become a silent one.

The scene ends with the two travelers fading out slowly in a lowering light of enveloping distance. In the shadows there is a sense of motion like an undulating sea. Gradual relighting reveals beggars, street people, lepers, naked mystics, snake charmers, rope tricksters, men, women, and children in still form as in the opening "miniature."

The merchant and his companion enter the scene. Suddenly a larger than life figure of the black goddess Kali is flashed against the background. She is crouched over her prone lover Shiva, her tongue out, arms extending, her torso garlanded with skulls on a large necklace. The merchant cries out in horror and fear, as voices of the people call out "Kali! Kali!"

ABULFULAN.   God! God! Help me!

POET.   She's in her mating season,
Her destroying season.
Shiva must satisfy her
To bring fertility and peace
Or she will kill him.

ABULFULAN.   God the Merciful and the Compassionate
Help me, O the Providing, the Protecting,
The Only One

POET.   See, the Penis is rising, look there!

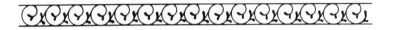

ABULFULAN.   I can't look.

   O my God, have mercy on this contrite heart.

The crowd sighs and wails as all stare awed at the imaged re-enactment. The goddess bleats wildly as the people groan in their suffering. The raging passion abates slowly until a quiet motion is restored. The image calms and fades.

ABULFULAN.   It is frightening!

POET.   It is wonderful.

ABULFULAN.   It is insane!

POET.   It is alive.

ABULFULAN.   These people have lost all reason.

POET.   They feel wonderfully crazy!

ABULFULAN.   I don't want them to touch me.

POET.   I want to run among them!

They are surrounded suddenly. The merchant screams for help, the poet in ecstasy. Their cries continue as they are carried off into the darkening crowd.

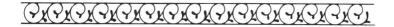

*The merchant and the poet reenter the stage at a
row of small shops, hawkers, et al. They address a
jewel seller, who is one-eyed.*

ABULFULAN.   Now stand to one side and let me speak.
I know these jewel sellers.

POET.   He looks wily. Are you sure he's trustworthy?

ABULFULAN.   His name was given by a friend.

POET.   A friend who's is your debt
Or out for your embarrassment?

ABULFULAN.   Why am I always accompanied by guides
Who think I need their guidance?
I am the patron, you the poet—remember that.

POET.   You find his eye appealing?

ABULFULAN.   No, disgusting. I wish he'd wear a patch
Over its cavity. These Hindus have no shame.
I'll look away.

POET.   No, he'll know you're shockable. You must be firm.
Look steadily into it to show you're not afraid.

Imagine you are looking into the navel of Zumurrad
And the emerald you seek is already there.

ABULFULAN. Ohhh.

POET. Practice the art of dissimulation perfected by our
people.
Let your eyes jitter back and forth to blur his face.
He'll never know your deeper feelings of disgust.

ABULFULAN. I hope advice will one day not be free
But taxed—excessively!
Sir. Jeweler. Sheth. You *are* Sheth?

SHETH. I am Sheth. At your service.

ABULFULAN. Hamid ud Din of Isfahan gave me your name.

SHETH. Yes, yes. My name is known. I'm pleased.

ABULFULAN. He said your emeralds are of the highest quality.

SHETH. He is too kind. You wish to see?

ABULFULAN. Yes. My favorite desires it above all else.

SHETH. I have the finest for her then.
See.

Sheth holds one up before his empty eye socket.
The merchant shivers, almost losing his food.

ABULFULAN [*staring intently, but shifting on his feet back and forth*]. It is good but I have seen better.

SHETH.   None better, none better.

ABULFULAN.   It is worth four gold pieces.

SHETH.   Ha ha ha ha . . .

ABULFULAN.   Five at most.

SHETH.   Ha! Thirty.

ABULFULAN.   What? Maybe it is worth six or seven
In Isfahan or Shiraz or eight in Baghdad.

SHETH.   Thirty is the lowest price,
And only for you whose friend is Hamid ud Din;
Fifty for another.

ABULFULAN [*aside to Poet*].   This is out of the question. These
Hindus are thieves.

POET.   Offer him ten. I think he'll take ten from you.

ABULFULAN.   Ten gold pieces!?

POET.   For Zumurrad's navel . . . after dinner . . .
   Shimmering with light before your liquid gaze . . .

ABULFULAN.   That's enough. I have to concentrate.

POET.   Think of his beard as her—

ABULFULAN.   Stop! I'll offer ten.
   Sheth, I can consider ten, no more.

SHETH.   Ha ha . . . Thirty!

POET.   Try fifteen. It will ride in her navel
   Like a ship on the sea, like a camel on a desert dune . . .

ABULFULAN.   Are you his ally or mine?
   Fifteen! No more.

SHETH.   Hamid ud Din from Isfahan?

ABULFULAN.   Yes.

SHETH.   I don't know him.

ABULFULAN.   What?

SHETH.   But that is no matter. Eighteen gold pieces.

ABULFULAN.   I said fifteen.

POET.   He will take sixteen, my patron,
     For this lovely adornment of your lover's navel.

ABULFULAN.   Sixteen.

SHETH.   All right, I will take seventeen.

ABULFULAN.   Seventeen?

SHETH.   Agreed!
     Would you be interested in silver?

ABULFULAN.   No.

> *He counts out gold pieces, takes jewel in hand,*
> *studies it, is pleased but cautious. He and the poet*
> *smile at each other and leave.*

SHETH.   These Arabs are queer indeed.
     Though they buy presents for women,
     Their eyes shake seductively when they gaze on men.
     Maybe that's why it is so easy to sell them false jewels . . . ?

95

The merchant and the poet companion alone.

ABULFULAN.　Where is my world?
　　I am not a traveler, my poet.
　　I miss my home, I like my home:
　　The faces on the bridge of boats,
　　The friendly people who hear my bell;
　　Our call to prayer, the Word of God intoned
　　Five times each day. Our life has order
　　Against this chaos and intrusion of humanity
　　In its obeisance to a false divinity.
　　I miss the sounds familiar to my ears.

POET.　We must return. You have your purchases.
　　Your work is almost done. You found
　　Your rival factions still at war;
　　Your weapons have sold well.
　　I think your heart tells you to leave.

ABULFULAN.　You're old enough to read the hearts of men?

POET.　It isn't age.

ABULFULAN.　Then wisdom.

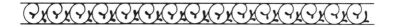

POET.   No. I have no wisdom, only age.

ABULFULAN.   Then something in the way you live.
I cannot read another's heart,
I cannot read my own.

POET.   It must be read by others when we cannot read.
We are wise when we accept the fact
That others read our hearts when we cannot
And foolish when we say that we alone can read them.

ABULFULAN.   What is the secret of your acceptance of that *fact*?

POET.   I am only your companion, not your spiritual guide.

ABULFULAN.   My heart is sad; can you cure that with words?

POET.   No. My words may change a mood but cannot cure a
heart.

ABULFULAN.   Then keep them to yourself.
I do not pay physicians who observe but will not risk
To treat my pain.

POET.   You are entitled to another's risk perhaps.
So I'll prescribe: we must return.

I see the heart is much too frail
To bear this distance any longer.

ABULFULAN.   Why am I not happy with this prescription?
I need others to look less sad.

POET.   You cannot expect others to enjoy your happiness
Though they may feel entitled to some of your pursuits.
Perhaps my own return is not to be a happy one.

ABULFULAN.   You are reading my heart now, not yours!

POET.   I'm speaking of the fear a traveler has
When leaving a world that's touched his soul
That he may not find that soul again at home.

ABULFULAN.   My heart says home. I'm tired of longing.

POET.   May our return be one of peace and joy at our reunions.

ABULFULAN.   Now I see a hint of happiness—just a hint—in
your eye
When you said reunions. That's what I want to see.

POET.   May light grow from that hint and you be joyous
In your radiant anticipation.

In a field in Khuhistan. Many birds are imaged as free, richly plumaged: on the ground, in grass, in trees. The merchant halts the caravan and separates from his companion and others to deliver his message directly to one of the birds. He makes sure he is alone, then walks among the birds, who withdraw from him cautiously. Finally, one steps forward and suddenly the merchant and this parrot are alone.

ABULFULAN.   When I left for Hindustan I asked my wives and servants what I might bring them each as a gift . . .

BIRD.   As a gift . . .

ABULFULAN.   Once I brought myself a gift . . .

BIRD.   Myself a gift . . .

ABULFULAN.   A parrot like yourself.

BIRD.   Like yourself . . .

ABULFULAN.   I asked him, too, what I could bring him from my journey.

BIRD.   My journey . . .

ABULFULAN.   He asked me only this: when I pass through the fields of Khuhistan and see his brothers living freely in

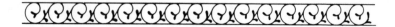

the meadows and the trees, I say to them a brother of theirs is imprisoned in a cage. Tell them he asks them to show him a way to find release from his cage. Is it just that he is filled with this desire in his soul while you are free? Is this the faith of friends?

The bird is silent this time, then is seized with anguish and pain, and in a moment falls down on the ground and lies still. The merchant recoils in horror, then comes forward to feel the body.

ABULFULAN.   My God, my God! He is dead. What is this . . . ? Is my nightingale in danger . . . ?

Poet and Caravan Master alone.

CARAVAN MASTER.   Four sunrises more, then celebrations.
It has been a successful journey.
We have not been robbed.
We have nothing left to fear
Now we are safely on our own terrain.

100

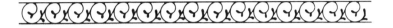

POET.   You are not a traveler.

CARAVAN MASTER.   What? Traveling is my business.

POET.   But you don't enjoy the other world
You cross into.

CARAVAN MASTER.   I enjoy. I know that other world,
The Hindus' land.
It has everything you'd ever want to see.
A cacophony of tongues and creeds,
Of rich and poor, of overfed and starving,
Of healthy and diseased,
Of princes in gold-threaded silks,
Of naked men who smear themselves with ashes.
Nothing remains itself that enters there.
Our God has not brought order to it yet
For reasons of His own.
The Merciful, the Compassionate
Knows what He is doing.

POET.   Our master is unhappy there.

CARAVAN MASTER.   He is a merchant,
Not the master of a caravan.
We are not the same.

He travels there to raise his wealth at home.
I do a job that carries me abroad
Because I have no wealth to keep at home.

POET.   He has not said a word for days.

CARAVAN MASTER.   It is the homesickness he has had before
Or the diarrhea from the foreign food and wells—
He gets it every time;
He has no stomach for the fiery spices.

POET.   His heart is filled with fears of loss.
He wants no company.

CARAVAN MASTER.   Four days more he'll have his company.
He'll place his emerald on the belly of Zumurrad
And watch it rise and fall like foam on the sea.

POET.   He looks like one whose eyes have long been blind.

CARAVAN MASTER.   He is this way each time he nears his home.
He has no eye for anything but what he thinks he'll see at
home.
It's nothing new.

POET.   I think it's new.
It's *not* homesickness—it's fear.

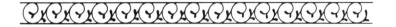

CARAVAN MASTER.   We won't be robbed.
   His goods are safe.
   I don't envision any loss.

POET.   He fears his loss has been
   While he was gone.

CARAVAN MASTER.   I checked all his possessions
   And check again each day.

POET.   Before he left for Hindustan.
   Before.
   He has the look of one whose life
   Keeps traveling and cannot stop,
   Whose life is not the life he thought he lived.
   It is his age perhaps
   To be afraid of loss.
   A little older
   And he'll yearn to give it all away
   Like the naked men who smear themselves with ashes:
   One day they might be seen as friends
   But now, to him, they terrify
   In their abandonment of all he thinks he needs.
   Fear and desire are like two brothers
   Not yet reconciled over their inheritance,
   Which in the end they both surrender

Yearning to be poor.
You say four sunrises left til their reconciliation?

CARAVAN MASTER.   Yes, four.

POET.   May The Light our God give Peace
And Compassionate illuminations to the number four.

The return scene is one of cries of jubilation, with women, children, servants running to greet, men with petitions assembling, Zumurrad in the window. He takes notice of the latter but without desire. He watches as they all scurry about receiving their gifts from various hands. He is preoccupied. He sees his black eunuch, rushes to him.

ABULFULAN.   Is he alive?

AHMAD.   Master, blessings and gratitude to God
For your safe return.

ABULFULAN.   Is he *alive?*

AHMAD.   Which *he*, what *alive?*

ABULFULAN.   My parrot, my parrot!

AHMAD.   We are all your parrots.
You are our master.

ABULFULAN.   My bird, damn you.
Tell me: is he alive?

AHMAD.   Oh, *that* parrot.
Yes, and silently awaiting your return.
He will not speak to anyone but you.
He knows whom he is kept to echo and amuse.

ABULFULAN.   I must see him to be sure.

AHMAD.   You do not trust me?

ABULFULAN.   I trust no one!
The gifts are here for everyone.
I'll leave them to their gifts.
That's all they want.

AHMAD.   They want you too.
Your wives and children,
Zumurrad there,
I, master, we all want you.

ABULFULAN.   I must see my only one
And no one else.

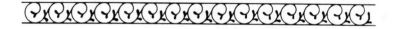

He leaves. The light dims on the reception. The merchant enters the private, inmost chamber where the bird stands inside the golden cage, uncovered since it is light. We hear the oud and reed pipe softly repeating the Bird's Theme.

ABULFULAN.   You are here—and alive!

BIRD.   Here—alive . . .

ABULFULAN.   I thought I had lost you,
    As if I had lost my very soul.

BIRD.   My very soul . . .

ABULFULAN.   Tell me something else but what I say myself;
    Tell me you are glad to see me.

BIRD.   Glad to see me . . .

ABULFULAN.   I am.
    Are you—to see me?

BIRD.   To see me . . .

ABULFULAN.   I brought the others gifts.

BIRD.   Gifts?

106

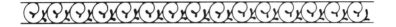

ABULFULAN. I am afraid to speak of yours.
[*The Bird is silent.*]
I did just what you asked,
But it was terrible what happened.

BIRD. Tell me what was terrible that happened.

ABULFULAN. I cannot.
I only want to be with you.
I only want to know you're safe,
To know you're here and I'm here,
To hear your voice as always.

BIRD. As always . . .

ABULFULAN. Can't you say anything to me but what I say?

BIRD. What I say . . .

ABULFULAN. Don't make me tell you.

BIRD. Tell you . . .

ABULFULAN. I've had a terrible journey.
I've suffered all I can suffer.
Too much has been inflicted upon me;
More than I can bear has been put on my back,

107

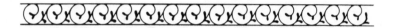

And God said he would burden but not break our backs.
Some men are suited for strangeness;
Some men can stand confusion; some men
Can be lost and alone and not feel threatened;
Some men's souls can survive without boundaries and
    definitions.
But mine, everything fastens to mine;
Everyone controls mine, but myself;
Everyone feels entitled to mine;
Everyone believes he is free to assault what is mine.
I am not meant to do what I do;
I am not meant to be who I am.
I am old, I feel old. Old age is upon me. I feel its ashes
On my hands, which shake,
On my lips, which tremble,
On my heart, which knows only fear.
Grant me the silence of our two presences together—
Quiet my heart, my lips, my hands.

BIRD.   Give me the gift you promised from your journey.

ABULFULAN.   I have nothing to give you.
   Listen to my heart.

BIRD.   I hear your heart.
   I have always heard your heart.

Tell me what happened
That made your hands shake, your lips tremble.

ABULFULAN. My soul cannot bear the words that would tell
you.

BIRD. Unburden your soul, release your words.

ABULFULAN. I am afraid, my heart is afraid.

BIRD. I can read your heart that's afraid.
Tell me what happened—
There is no other way to end your fear.
Give me the gift that you promised me.

ABULFULAN. I am afraid I will lose you.
If I lose you, I have lost my soul.

BIRD. Speak!

ABULFULAN. Speak?

BIRD. Speak to me.

ABULFULAN. Speak to me!

BIRD. Tell me exactly what happened.

ABULFULAN.   Exactly what happened . . .
  I told your brother in the field
  What you had told me to tell him—
  That a brother of his was imprisoned in a cage,
  That he should remember you when he was free
  In his meadow and his trees. I told him
  You asked him to show you a way to find release
  From your cage.

BIRD.   What did he do then? Tell me.

ABULFULAN.   He began to shake all over. His eyes rolled in his
      head.
  He fell down on the ground and lay still. I went in fright
  To touch his body. He was cold. He was—dead.
  [*Cries, shakes with fear*].

BIRD [*Silent. After a pause, begins to shake*].

ABULFULAN.   No!

BIRD [*His shaking becomes violent*].

ABULFULAN.   No!

BIRD [*His eyes roll, he falls down in his cage, lies still*].

ABULFULAN. No, no, no, no, no . . .
[*Cries helplessly*] My heart cannot stand . . .
God, you said you would not break us . . .
I cannot live without my soul . . .

The merchant becomes angry after moments of
wordless anguish.

ABULFULAN. God! God!

He opens the cage with his key. He takes the bird in his arms,
carries its limp body to a window, weeping, cursing, throws
it (with the help of invisible wires) away into the outer court-
yard. The bird instantly takes flight, surges upward to the top
of a tree. He pauses in silence looking down at his former
captor.

ABULFULAN. What have you done to me?
Speak to me!

BIRD. We are brothers, not creatures to be put in cages.
My brother taught me by his silent act
My own voice kept me a prisoner.
We are two bodies, he and I, but one soul.

ABULFULAN. Don't leave me—
I will leave the door of the cage always open,

111

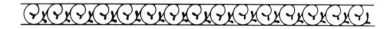

I will treat you well,
Speak to me . . .
Give me something I can hold . . .

> *The Bird looks down as if to speak but then extends its wings and without further words flies away.*

ABULFULAN [*devastated*].   Where is my soul?

THREE POEMS

THRESHOLD

i

He sinned with me a pleasant sin.* Dear God,
We loved too suddenly. We touched, we dove
Beneath the waves, our childish dreams washed off,
And out we walked alive to love. I don't
Regret, but now each year is longer than
The last. I wait in doorways knowing he
Has left. My cheeks are raw. The threshold just
Leads in and out; life's inconclusive to itself.
The one who loved too much to leave is now
A dream another left behind. I still
Can't sleep alone. I hunger for him just
To sleep. How should I rest in paradise?*
I have this room, this chair, this rug he bought.
I ask You only if it's years and years.

ii

I never knew if he had found new faith
Or lost the old again—I mean, each day

*from Christina Rossetti's *The Convent Threshold*

115

When we awoke and called. What was his mood?
I never could predict: I want to die
And yet I know I only want to live.
The time between his inner states was short,
So short I couldn't tell if lost was found
Or hopelessness was hope. The matter was
Religious, he believed, or was it dread
Of waking up alone or not alone?
He didn't want the problem solved or did.
He wanted quiet, but then he needed noise.
He wanted time; time came, it was too much.
And then he looked for someone else to love.

iii

I start by waking up at night: a scent,
A sound, a touch, a dream that's too direct.
I cry. I stare at two red eyes. I call.
I think I hear a voice, his voice; the musk,
His scent, returns. I feel his hard resolving chest
Against my breasts and then I know he's gone.
Am I possessed? I offered nothing less
Than all I felt and thought and all I longed
To be. I wanted love, not studied love;
I wanted struggled for, not wasted, words;
I wanted grace to dance. Each day begins
And ends with moments that have come and gone
We barely grasped, like mists or dins of birds,
Each only free of havoc when in flight.

BEC VILIN

A Breton tower on the Côte du Nord near Plougrescant,
visited after the Seven Sleepers Pilgrimage in Vieux Marché.

The sound of sea, the breathing that calls
The soul to come away, to become driftwood
Leaving the alewife and her ways of love.
The wound is washed incessantly.

I turn around like a startled fish
To seize what I did not expect
Coming at the end of all its witnesses
Saying patience, patience softly in its streets;

Faces coming toward me in the darkness
Carrying candles and rising
From their early sleep.

'O in love we are very high, but nailed;
Free, but caught . . .'

My eyes flow like those persons
Through the fires and the weeds.
Their Word was once conceived by hearing,
Now nothing in the midnight prompts.

117

The building is filled with fallen rocks
And grass and vines like an underground man
Struggling to possess his victim's treasure.

That is all I have of either:
A scandal; poverty; bankruptcy; wind
Through a skeleton, through a megalithic city.
All poetry finds its grace:

A black butterfly flies in a window
And flies out again.

CRUEL MUSE

A cruel muse, the daemon wakes me
When I'm well-disposed to sleep:
You are here to be and to love,
To let your life unfold,
Not to withdraw and rest.

And so I rise out of a half-used bed
To look out at the cove.
I hear men curse the lobster traps they set,
And watch gulls hang in air
And make their solitary piercing cries
As if tied always to their fears.

Lights flicker on. Awake,
I have to agonize for stillness.
I turn to love and ask or plead:
Am I a piece of old dry wood,
An object to consume,
That cries its flesh out in a fire?

I have no other voice to trust.